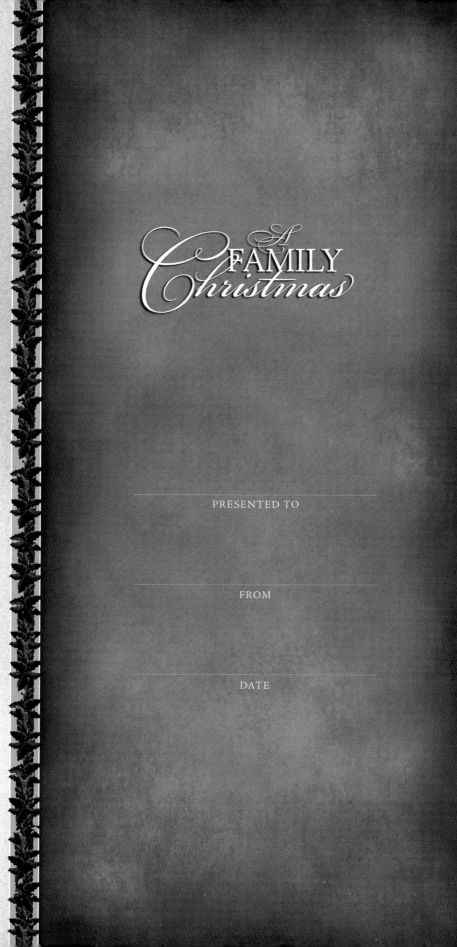

A FAMILY Christmas

_____

PRESENTED TO

_____

FROM

_____

DATE

This book is affectionately dedicated to families that are striving to raise healthy children in a topsy-turvy and often bewildering world. I hope the touching stories and beautiful reproductions of G. Harvey's paintings will provide renewed inspiration as you celebrate the birth of the Christ child.

All meaning and purpose in life are rooted in that blessed event!

Merry Christmas, one and all.

James Dobson

To my family and friends, who have enriched my life,
and ultimately to the Lord,
who has given us the greatest blessing—
allowing us to be a part of His family.

G. Harvey

Dr. James Dobson

A FAMILY Christmas

With Paintings by
G. HARVEY

Multnomah Gifts™

Multnomah® Publishers *Sisters, Oregon*

A Family Christmas
© 2002 by James Dobson, Inc.
published by Multnomah Gifts™,
a division of Multnomah® Publishers, Inc.
P.O. Box 1720, Sisters, Oregon 97759

ISBN 1-57673-924-4

Artwork by G. Harvey. All artwork contributed for *A Family Christmas* is
an original creation of G. Harvey's and ownership of all images or images
reproduced from *A Family Christmas* are the exclusive property of and
copyrighted to and in the name of G. Harvey, LTD and G. Harvey, Inc.

Designed by Koechel Peterson & Associates, Mpls., MN

Please see the acknowledgments at the back of the book for complete
attributions for this material.

Scripture quotations are taken from *The Holy Bible*, New International Version
© 1973, 1984 by International Bible Society, used by permission of Zondervan
Publishing House; *The Holy Bible*, New King James Version (NKJV) © 1984
by Thomas Nelson, Inc.

Multnomah is a trademark of Multnomah Publishers, Inc., and is registered
in the U.S. Patent and Trademark Office. The colophon is a trademark of
Multnomah Publishers, Inc.

Library of Congress Cataloging-in-Publication Data

Dobson, James C., 1936-
    A family Christmas / by James Dobson / art by G. Harvey.
        p. cm.
    ISBN 1-57673-924-4 (hardcover)
    1. Christmas. I. Title.
    BV45 .D59 2002
    242'.335—dc21   2002004811

Printed in Belgium

TABLE of CONTENTS

Introduction 5

Delayed Delivery 9

Holy Awakenings at Christmas 19

Christmas Lost and Found 27

A Christmas World 37

If You're Missing Baby Jesus 45

The Broken Ballerina 55

The Town That Gave Christmas 65

The Christmas Story 75

INTRODUCTION

— ✦ —

What three words in our language carry more

emotionally laden memories than "A Family Christmas"?

What other simple phrase unleashes such a flood of nostalgia,

half-forgotten longings, and well-remembered tastes,

smells, sounds, melodies, and images?

A Family Christmas.

Happy or sad, festive or quiet, "A Family Christmas"

carries us from where we are to where we've been...or perhaps

where we want to be. I have only to close my eyes to find myself

in scenes of my boyhood in Texas with my father and mother—

scenes that are often interwoven with images from Oklahoma,

California, and Kansas…around the fireplace with Shirley, Danae, and Ryan…lights low, the fire popping and snapping on the grate, and the sweet fragrance of Christmas candles filling the room. These are among the most precious moments of my life.

A Family Christmas.

There are other yuletide images that most of us have only seen in literature, art, and film. They represent a time gone by, before most of us were born. And yet, they are part of the heritage of Christmas that is still with us today. Through the work of gifted artists such as my dear friend Gerald Harvey, many of these turn-of-the-century scenes are vividly preserved on canvas and in sculpture. Sleighs jingling along snowy country lanes; the clip-clop of horse hooves on cobbled streets; the soft glow of gas lights around a town square filled with shoppers;

and tiny churches on starry nights, light pouring from the
windows and the good folks of the village gathering for a Christmas
Eve service of carols and praise. It is all there for us to enjoy.

A Family Christmas.

Whether we speak of our own families or the worldwide
family of God, this season is a time of giving and receiving like
no other. On the pages that follow, you will find not only beautiful
reproductions of G. Harvey's work, but a collection of favorite
stories of Christmases Past. We hope they will bring
rekindled warmth and joy to you and yours.

Emmanuel! God is with us!

— ❧ —

James Dobson

Delayed DELIVERY

There had never been a winter like this. Stella watched from the haven of her armchair as gusts of snow whipped themselves into frenzy. She feared to stand close to the window, unreasonably afraid that somehow the blizzard might be able to reach her there, sucking her, breathless, out into the chaos. The houses across the street were all but obliterated by the fury of wind-borne flakes. Absently, the elderly woman straightened the slipcovers on the arms of her chair, her eyes glued to the spectacle beyond the glass.

CATHY
MILLER

*Christmas in
My Heart*

*"The virgin will be with child
and will give birth to a son, and they will
call him Immanuel"—which means,
"God with us."*

MATTHEW 1:23

9

Dragging her gaze away from the window, she forced herself up out of her chair and waited a moment for balance to reassert itself. Straightening her back against the pain that threatened to keep her stooped, she set out determinedly for the kitchen.

In the doorway to the next room she paused, her mind blank, wondering what purpose had propelled her there. From the vent above the stove the scream of the wind threatened to funnel the afternoon storm directly down into the tiny house. Stella focused brown eyes on the stovetop clock. The three-fifteen time reminded her that she had headed in there to take something out of the freezer for her supper. Another lonely meal that she didn't feel like preparing, much less eating.

Suddenly, she grabbed the handle of the refrigerator and leaned her forehead against the cool, white surface of the door as a wave of self-pity threatened to drown her. It was too much to bear, losing her beloved Dave this summer! How was she to endure the pain, the daily nothingness? She felt the familiar ache in her throat and squeezed her eyes tightly shut to hold the tears at bay.

Stella drew herself upright and shook her head in silent chastisement. She reiterated her litany of thanks. She had her health, her tiny home, an income that should suffice for the remainder of her days. She had her books, her television programs, her needlework. There were the pleasures of her garden in the spring and summer, walks through the wilderness park at the end of her street, and the winter birds that brightened the feeders outside her kitchen picture window. Not today though, she thought ruefully, as the blizzard hurled itself against the eastern wall of the kitchen.

"Ah, Dave, I miss you so! I never minded storms when you were here." The sound of her own voice echoed hollowly in the room. She turned on the radio that stood on the counter next to a neatly descending row of wooden canisters. A sudden joyful chorus of Christmas music filled the room, but it only served to deepen her loneliness.

Stella had been prepared for her husband's death. Since the doctor's pronouncement of terminal lung cancer, they had both faced the inevitable, striving to make the most of their remaining time together. Dave's financial affairs had always been in order. There were no new burdens in her widowed state. It was just the awful aloneness…the lack of purpose to her days.

They had been a childless couple. It had been their choice. Their lives had been full and rich. They had been content with busy careers, and with each other. They had had many friends. Had. That was the operative word these days. It was bad enough losing the one person you loved with all your heart. But over the past few years, she and Dave repeatedly had to cope with the deaths of their friends and relations. They were all of an age—the age when human bodies began giving up—dying. Face it—they were old!

And no, on this first Christmas without Dave, Stella would be on her own. Mable and Jim had invited her to spend the holiday with them in Florida, but somehow that had seemed worse than staying at home alone. Not only would she miss her husband, but she would miss the snow and the winter and the familiarity of her home.

With shaky fingers, she lowered the volume of the radio so that the music became a muted background. She glanced toward the fridge briefly, then decided that a hot bowl of soup would be more comforting fare this evening.

To her surprise, she saw that the mail had come. She hadn't even heard the creak of the levered mail slot in the front door. Poor mailman, out in this weather! "Nor hail, nor sleet…" With the inevitable wince of pain, she bent to retrieve the damp white envelopes from the floor. Moving into the

living room, she sat on the piano bench to open them. They were mostly Christmas cards, and her sad eyes smiled at the familiarity of the traditional scenes and at the loving messages inside. Carefully, her arthritic fingers arranged them among the others clustered on the piano top. In her entire house, they were the only seasonal decoration. The holiday was less than a week away, but she just did not have the heart to put up a silly tree, or even set up the stable that Dave had built with his own hands.

Suddenly engulfed by the loneliness of it all, Stella buried her lined face in her hands, lowering her elbows to the piano keys in a harsh, abrasive discord, and let the tears come. How would she possibly get through Christmas and the winter beyond it? She longed to climb into bed and bury herself in a cocoon of blankets, not emerging until her friends and spring returned.

The ring of the doorbell echoed the high-pitched, discordant piano notes and was so unexpected that Stella had to stifle a small scream of surprise. Now who could possibly be calling on her on a day like today? Wiping her eyes, she noticed for the first time how dark the room had become. The doorbell sounded a second time.

Using the piano for leverage, she raised herself upright and headed for the front hall, switching on the living room light as she passed. She opened the wooden door and stared through the screened window of the storm door in consternation. On her front porch, buffeted by waves of wind and snow, stood a strange young man, whose hatless head was barely visible above the large carton in his arms. She peered beyond him to the driveway, but there was nothing about the small car to give clue to his identity. Returning her gaze to him, she saw that his hands were bare and his eyebrows had lifted in an expression of hopeful appeal that was fast disappearing behind the frost forming on the glass. Summoning courage, the elderly lady opened the door slightly and he stepped sideways to speak into the space.

"Mrs. Thornhope?"

She nodded in affirmation, her extended

THERE IS A BETTER THING

than the observance of Christmas Day,

and that is keeping Christmas.

Are you willing...

To believe that love

is the strongest thing in the world?

Stronger than hate? Stronger than death?

And that the blessed Life which began

in Bethlehem nineteen hundred years ago

is the image and brightness of eternal love?

Then you can keep Christmas!

HENRY VAN DYKE

13

arm beginning to tremble with cold and the strain of holding the door against the wind. He spoke again. "I have a package for you."

Curiosity drove warning thoughts from her mind. She pushed the door far enough to enable the stranger to shoulder it and stepped back into the foyer to make room for him. He entered, bringing with him the frozen breath of the storm. Smiling, he placed his burden carefully on the floor and stood to retrieve an envelope that protruded from his pocket. As he handed it to her, a sound came from the box. Stella actually jumped. The man laughed in apology and bent to straighten up the cardboard flaps, holding them open in an invitation for her to peek inside. She advanced cautiously, then turned her gaze downward.

It was a dog! To be more exact, a golden Labrador retriever puppy. As the gentleman lifted its squirming body up into his arms, he explained, "This is for you, ma'am. He's six weeks old and completely housebroken." The young pup wiggled in happiness at being released from captivity and thrust ecstatic, wet kisses in the direction of his benefactor's chin. "We were supposed to deliver him on Christmas Eve," he continued with some difficulty, and he strove to rescue his chin from the wet little tongue, "but the staff at the kennels start their holidays tomorrow. Hope you don't mind an early present."

Shock had stolen her ability to think clearly. Unable to form coherent sentences, she stammered, "but…I don't…I mean… who…?"

The young fellow set the animal down on the doormat between them and then reached out a finger to tap the envelope she was still holding.

"There's a letter in there that explains everything, pretty much. The dog was bought last July while her mother was still pregnant. It was meant to be a Christmas gift. If you'll just wait a minute, there are some things in the car I'll get for you."

Before she could protest, he was gone, returning a moment later with a huge box of dog food, a leash, and a book entitled *Caring for Your Labrador Retriever*. All this time the puppy had sat quietly at her feet, panting happily as his brown eyes watched her.

Unbelievably, the stranger was turning to go. Desperation forced the words from her lips. "But who…who bought it?"

Pausing in the open doorway, his words almost snatched away by the wind that tousled his hair, he replied, "Your husband, ma'am." And then he was gone.

It was all in the letter. Forgetting the puppy entirely at this sight of the familiar handwriting, Stella had walked like a somnambulist to her chair by the window. Unaware that the little dog had followed her, she forced tear-filled eyes to read her husband's words. He had written it three weeks before his death and had left it with the kennel owners to be delivered along with

the puppy as his last Christmas gift to her. It was full of love and encouragement and admonishments to be strong. He vowed that he was waiting for the day when she would join him. And he had sent her this young animal to keep her company until then.

Remembering the little creature for the first time, she was surprised to find him quietly looking up at her, his small panting mouth resembling a comic smile. Stella put the pages aside and reached down for the bundle of golden fur. She thought that he would be heavier, but he was only the size and weight of a sofa pillow. And so soft and warm. She cradled him in her arms and he

licked her jawbone, then cuddled up into the hollow of her neck. The tears began anew at this exchange of affection and the dog endured her crying without moving.

Finally, Stella lowered him to her lap, where he regarded her solemnly. She wiped vaguely at her wet cheeks, then somehow mustered a smile.

"Well, little guy, I guess it's up to you and me." His pink tongue panted in agreement. Stella's smile strengthened and her gaze shifted sideways to the window. Dusk had fallen, and the storm seemed to have spent the worst of its fury. Through fluffy flakes that were now drifting down at a gentler pace, she saw the cheery Christmas lights that edged the rooflines of her neighbors'

homes. The strains of "Joy to the World" wafted in from the kitchen.

Suddenly Stella felt the most amazing sensation of peace and benediction washing over her. It was like being enfolded in a loving embrace. Her heart beat painfully, but it was with joy and wonder, not grief or loneliness. She need never feel alone again. Returning her attention to the dog, she spoke to him, "You know, fella, I have a box in the basement that I think you'd like. There's a tree in it and some decorations and lights that will impress you like crazy! And I think I can find that old stable down there, too. What d'ya say we go hunt it up?" The puppy barked happily in agreement, as if he understood every word.

LOVE IS STRONGER THAN DEATH *and reaches*

into eternity. Gifts of kindness, given from loving hearts, can warm

the coldest winter and bring light into dark and lonely places.

And once upon a dark night in a little village called Bethlehem,

every one of us received a Gift like no other. It was a Gift of surpassing

kindness and enduring love… a Gift that to this day warms hearts,

releases captives, pushes back the shadows, and delivers hope

and joy to transform desolate seasons of our lives.

God's great Gift, delivered just when we needed it most,

will walk with us through every trial, every hardship, every lonely day,

and every starless night. And one day we'll all be together in the presence

of the Gift, where loneliness and death and separation

and tears will fade like a distant dream.

The Gift is ours, right now. And His name is Jesus.

— ❧ —

James Dobson

Holy Awakenings
AT CHRISTMAS

*I*t was Thursday morning, the first week of December. In keeping with family tradition, I hauled the dusty Christmas boxes from the attic and set out to fill our little home with the holiday spirit. Eager as a child in a candy store, I flung open cartons, inspected breakables, and gently removed the dilapidated nativity from its nest of white tissue paper. Slowly I counted each ragged piece, carefully assembled it, and placed it on one end of the hearth, daring anyone to touch it.

DAYLE
ALLEN
SHOCKLEY

*Whispers
from Heaven*

*We have seen his glory,
the glory of the One and Only,
who came from the Father,
full of grace and truth.*

JOHN 1:14

19

Although this particular nativity is probably the least expensive item in my growing collection of Christmas decorations, its worth is immeasurable to me. My mother and I both grew up with this cardboard crèche. At least sixty years old, it continues to bring me pleasure year after year.

As a young girl, I remember crouching in front of the manger scene, my eyes mesmerized by the Virgin Mary. Wrapped in a pale blue robe, a glow about her head, she appeared so holy and beautiful to me.

Smiling at the familiar faces of the shepherds and wise men, I steadied them in their corner of the stable, giving each a gentle pat. The beloved nativity now belonged to me. One day I would pass it on to my child.

Later in the day, I showed the nativity to my daughter—who was barely two at the time—and carefully related the splendid story of Christmas, using the cardboard figures to illustrate the narrative.

Anna pointed to the wise men.

"Those are the three wise men," I said. "They've come to bring the baby Jesus gifts. See?" Holding up one of the wise men, I let her inspect the small parcel in his hands. Satisfied, she scooted off my lap and down the hall.

Over the next couple of days, I draped the house with trinkets and fresh holly, with wreaths and berry-scented candles, creating the cozy, country charm I find so appealing. I felt quite pleased with my talents.

On Sunday afternoon, I dashed through the house—gathering up the few things

I had not used in my decorating spree—and found Sunshine lying at the edge of the cardboard nativity. Sunshine was Anna's shabby doll, the one she loved more than all of her toys combined. The doll's frazzled appearance attested to that fact. Faltering eyelids. Limp body. Only one unruly strand of hair remaining.

This was not the first time I had found the doll dangerously close to the fragile crèche. Clearly, something must be done. Glancing at my daughter, I gently inquired, "What is Sunshine doing here, sweetie?"

"Jesus," she said steadily, her eyes watching me like a hawk. "Jesus," she repeated, giving her head a rather curt nod.

Jesus? Sunshine was Jesus? This was not going to be easy. I could hardly dismiss Jesus from the scene without some explanation. But Anna spoke only a few words. How would I make her understand that this nativity was precious decoration, not something to play with?

"So Sunshine is baby Jesus?"

Anna shook her head no. "Jesus!" she said again, this time with clear passion.

I stared dumbly at the doll. If Sunshine was not baby Jesus, then I didn't have a clue. "Well look, Anna," I coaxed, "Mommy and Daddy are expecting company tonight. I don't think Sunshine should be here. Besides, this is not a toy." I pointed to the cardboard nativity. "OK?"

Her face fell. Appearing most disheartened, Anna took the doll and disappeared around the corner, leaving me staring after her in silent wonder and feeling horribly guilty. Had I become too caught up in decorating for the holidays? What was my motive here? And how could I be so insensitive to my precious child? Where was my Christmas spirit anyway?

AWAY IN A MANGER,

no crib for His bed,

The little Lord Jesus laid down His sweet head;

The stars in the sky looked down where He lay,

The little Lord Jesus, asleep on the hay.

BE NEAR ME LORD JESUS,

I ask Thee to stay,

Close by me forever, and love me I pray;

Bless all the dear children in Thy tender care,

And take us to glory, to live with Thee there.

MARTIN LUTHER

Unwilling to answer such questions, I cast them to the back of my mind.

Company came and went, and early next morning, I paused at the nativity. A pink strip of sun streamed through the window, casting a rosy hue over the face of the Christ child. And there, in front of the stable, much to my dismay, lay Sunshine—one eye opened, one eye closed.

So much for my guilt. I was instantly annoyed that my child had disobeyed my earlier request to keep Sunshine out of the manger scene. "Anna, please come here," I called, not a little perturbed.

In she toddled, tiny feet peeking out from under a polka-dotted gown. I pointed to the doll. "It would really be nice, sweetheart," I said, careful not to scold, "if you would keep Sunshine away from the nativity, like I asked you to. You might accidentally knock everything over," I told her, hoping that fact justified my behavior.

"Jesus," Anna said softly, her little head tilted to one side, her eyes pleading.

My heart ached. Stooping down, I pulled her close, determined to get to the bottom of this. "Why do you keep putting Sunshine here, sweetheart? You say she is not baby Jesus…"

She shook her head no.

"Well, then—"

"For Jesus," she said, haltingly.

"For Jesus," I mumbled, desperate to understand. "For Jesus."

As I contemplated her words, Anna wiggled from my hold, marched straight to the three wise men and pointed to their gifts. And that is when it hit me. "Oh! I see!"

I said, the truth finally sinking in. "Sunshine is your gift to the baby Jesus. Like the wise men. Right?

Her face beaming, she nodded, contented at last.

I gazed long and hard at Sunshine's exhausted body. Not a pretty gift at all. A definite liability to the nativity. Yet when I looked into my child's shining face, I realized that she had relinquished her most prized possession—the thing dearest to her heart. She had given sacrificially, just as God gave to the world on that first Christmas night.

Suddenly my hands felt empty, my heart heavy. What gift had I brought to this holy gathering?

Anna bent to take the doll away.

"No," I said, resolved. "She can stay."

I thought of the stirring words in Phillips Brooks's carol: "O holy Child of Bethlehem! Descend to us, we pray. Cast out our sin, and enter in. Be born in us today."

In the pink light of heaven, I knelt at my daughter's modest shrine. I sensed that she had come nearer to the heart of Christmas than I ever could hope to be.

HOW ODD TO THINK *that a toddler—*

scarcely two Christmases old—might grasp with tiny fingers

a truth that eludes many of us for years.

"For Jesus." For Him…our best, our heart, our all.

Our choicest treasures and dearest dreams.

The first hour of our morning and the quiet moments of twilight.

The best of our time, the best of our strength, the best of our talents,

the best of our years. And always, the best of our love.

Little Anna left her Sunshine—

her best friend and companion—alongside the manger.

And what shall we leave at His feet?

— ❧ —

James Dobson

Christmas Lost *and* Found

A lonely college freshman walked along the streets of Philadelphia on the day before Christmas 1975. Three weeks earlier his mother had written to break the news. The family could not afford to bring him home for the holidays. His father's business was in trouble, and there was no extra money for travel. That meant William Lambert would be forced to remain at the University of Pennsylvania during the entire Christmas season.

DANAE DOBSON

Christmas by the Hearth

"Ask and it will be given to you;
seek and you will find;
knock and the door will be opened to you."

MATTHEW 7:7

The winter break had been the most depressing period of William's life. With the exception of a foreign student who spoke little English, all the guys in his dormitory had left two weeks earlier in a flurry of activity. They talked excitedly about their moms' cooking and the families that awaited them back home. William had watched them pack and leave, feeling like the most wretched person on earth. His pain had become almost unbearable by that cold morning before Christmas.

Not even God knows that I'm alive, he thought to himself. If He cares, why didn't He help me get home for the holidays?

The question went unanswered.

In desperation, William boarded a bus for downtown Philly, hoping to find relief from his terrible loneliness. He pulled his collar around his neck to protect against the

bitter wind and walked along the decorated streets. The laughing, happy people reminded him of his friends at home in Idaho. He thought of his mother's traditional turkey dinner and the family sitting around the Christmas tree. How his heart longed to be with them at that moment.

In his wallet he carried a crisp $50 bill, a present from his parents. He knew they had sacrificed to send it to him. The card had said, "Buy something special for yourself," but nothing sounded appealing.

William spent most of the day wandering aimlessly in and out of stores. It somehow helped to be surrounded by crowds. Then, late in the afternoon, his vision suddenly focused. There in a shop window was an electric train chugging through a tiny frontier town. In front of the window was a young boy, about nine years old, standing transfixed in front of the glass. It was as though he were hypnotized by the train.

William was reminded of his own childhood in Boise. There was a toy store near his house, where he had stood and longed for a beautiful Lionel train. He knew his father could not afford such an expensive gift, but he secretly hoped for a miracle that never came. Now he recognized that same disappointment in the face of the boy before him. The lad walked away, casting one last glance over his shoulder.

Why not? William thought to himself.

He strolled over to the boy and tapped him on the shoulder. "Hi! My name is William," he said.

"I'm David," said the boy.

"That's a beautiful train, isn't it?"

"Yeah," said David. "It's the best train I've ever seen."

"How would you like to have that train?" he said to his young friend.

The boy's eyes widened. "Oh, I could never own it," he said. "We couldn't—I mean, my mom doesn't have very much money."

"Come on," said William, leading David into the store.

William knew that his motives might be misunderstood by someone older than David, but he meant no harm to the boy.

Indeed, this might have been the most unselfish moment of his life. Since he couldn't be a child again, he could at least enjoy making a boy's dream come true.

The salesclerk approached them and asked if he could be of help.

"That train in the window," William inquired. "How much is it—the whole set?"

"I believe it's about $50," he answered. "Let me check." In a few moments he returned to the counter. "It's $46.95. And worth every penny."

"That sounds terrific," William said. "We'll take it."

The salesclerk made his way to the storage room.

"Wow!" said David. "Do you really mean it? The train's for me? It's really mine?"

William gave the boy a pat on the shoulder and smiled.

"Hey," said David. "I live just around the corner. Wanna meet my mom? She's a really neat lady. I want her to meet you."

After William paid for the train, David said excitedly, "Come on! I wanna show Mom."

WHEN IT'S CHRISTMAS,

man is bigger and is better in his part;

He is keener for the service that is prompted by the heart.

All the petty thoughts and narrow

seem to vanish for awhile

And the true reward he's seeking is the glory of a smile.

Then for others he is toiling and somehow it seems to me

That at Christmas he is almost

what God wanted him to be.

EDGAR GUEST

William struggled to carry the box and keep track of the boy who ran ahead. A block away they came to an old brick building. David ran up a dark staircase and pounded on the door marked "201." An apron-clad woman in her 30s soon appeared.

"Mom," said David. "This man is my friend. He bought me a new train. Can he come in, Mom? Huh? Please?"

William tried to maneuver the box so he could see the woman. "Hi," he said. "I'm William Lambert. I hope you don't mind what I've done. I saw David looking at this train, and I could see how much he wanted it. I would really be pleased if you would let him accept it."

"Well, sure," said David's mother. "Bring it on in. My name is Pauline Sanders. You'll have to pardon me. I'm not used to having my son bring people home with him."

"I'll be leaving in a minute," said William. "I just wanted to help David carry the box home."

"No, no," said Pauline, seeing the kindness in the young man's eyes. "Come on in."

Her warm reaction reminded William of his own mother, who would have responded the same way if he had shown up at the door with a stranger.

"Won't you have a seat?" Pauline asked.

As William removed his hat and coat, he noticed the humble surroundings. The living room was clean and neat, although simple in appearance. A fire crackled in the hearth, and a small Bible lay on top of the coffee table. In the corner stood a frail Christmas tree, covered with popcorn strings and red ribbon. He noticed there were hardly any presents underneath.

David grabbed William's hand. "Don't sit down," he said. "First come see my room."

As they made their way down the hall, Pauline called from the kitchen. "Son, did you remember to pick up those apples for me?"

"They're on the counter, Mom," David replied. He then opened the door to a tiny bedroom. "This is my room," he said proudly.

"Very impressive," William remarked, looking around.

Two posters hung on the walls, and a few

model trains were displayed on the dresser.

"Did you make those models?" asked William.

"Yes," answered David. "All by myself!"

William picked up one of the trains and looked at it closely. "You did a good job," he said. "Better than I could have done."

David beamed with pride as they walked back to the kitchen.

"As long as you're here," Pauline said, "why don't you join us for Christmas dinner? It's just David and me. It'll be good to have a guest with us."

She had prepared a bountiful meal of turkey, mashed potatoes, and green beans. It was clearly a sacrificial tribute that had been extracted from a small budget. William smelled the food and said he would be delighted to stay.

"Do you mind if we say grace before we eat?" asked Pauline. "David and I are Christians."

"Really?" said William. "I'm a new Christian, too. I became a believer last month at an InterVarsity meeting, but there's still a lot I don't understand."

They bowed their heads while Pauline thanked God for His blessings and for the birth of His Son, Jesus.

During the meal, Pauline talked about her late husband, Richard. He had died in Vietnam five years before. She had wanted to leave Philadelphia ever since his death, preferring to live on the West Coast with her family.

"Someday," she said, "we'll be able to move. That's my dream."

"Why didn't you visit your family this Christmas?" asked William. Immediately he regretted asking.

Pauline sighed. "I really wanted to," she said, "but I just didn't have the money this year."

William explained that he, too, had wanted to go home for Christmas, but financial woes had kept him in Philly.

"Then it must be God's will that you're here tonight," Pauline noted.

William smiled. "It must be," he agreed.

After dinner, William and David sat on the floor and began putting the train set together. Pauline served apple dumplings as they talked and laughed and told stories.

Finally, after three hours, the task was finished. William sat back in a worn easy chair. "All right, David, start 'er up," he instructed.

The young boy reached for the control and pressed the button. In a flash the train was on its way, winding around the tracks with an occasional whistle blow.

The joy-filled expression on David's face was worth every penny William had spent. It was a feeling of immeasurable satisfaction knowing he had been able to make a boy happy at Christmas. After the train had made fifteen circuits, William announced he needed to get back to the university.

"I've had a wonderful evening," he said. "Thank you so much for making me feel at home. And the meal was delicious!"

"Wait just a minute," David pleaded. He ran from the room.

As William put on his coat and hat, he noticed that Pauline had tears in her eyes.

"I want you to know I've been praying the entire month for a way to buy David a nice Christmas present," she whispered.

"Your kindness was not only a gift to David but also to me. It was an answer to prayer."

Before William could respond, David rushed back into the living room. He was holding a little white box in his arms. "Merry Christmas, William," he said joyfully.

As William lifted the lid, he was surprised to see the model train David had shown him earlier surrounded by crumpled tissue paper.

"It's not as good as the one you gave me," David apologized, "but at least we both got a new train set for Christmas."

William reached out and gave his new friend a hug. "David, this is the nicest thing anyone ever gave me," he said.

A certain sadness came over William as he turned to leave. He knew he might never see the Sanderses again. Pauline and David thanked him for coming and for the gift, but William was the grateful one.

As he made his way to the bus stop, he reflected on all that had happened. He had found more satisfaction in his new friendships than in any Christmas celebration of the past. The words of Jesus, which he had learned as a child, rang in his ears. It really was more blessed to give than to receive!

As William rode the bus through the night, the meaning of the evening suddenly became clear—like a picture coming into focus. He and his new friends had each experienced a personal crisis before their chance encounter. Pauline had been on her knees, praying desperately for a gift to offer her fatherless son. Her little boy had longed for a prize that could never be his. And William had ached with unspeakable loneliness and despair. It was an impossible array of problems. There was no way, short of a miracle, that each set of needs could have been met simultaneously and in such a satisfying way. And yet it happened.

Could it be that a loving and compassionate Lord had been watching them on that day? Had He seen their distress and heard the longings of their heart? Did He bring them together to provide kindness to one another on Christmas Eve?

"Yes," murmured William to himself. "He does care. He is there!"

"Happy Birthday, Jesus," he said as he entered the quiet dorm. "And thank you." Then he added, "But next year—could I celebrate in Boise?"

THERE IS NO "IMPOSSIBLE ARRAY *of problems*" *greater*

than our God's ability to help and bless His dearly loved children.

He longs to bless us, and the Bible tells us that He inclines

His ear, bending low to hear the faintest prayer of the weakest believer.

Through a string of small miracles the world might call "coincidence,"

God works through the mystery of prayer

to meet our desires and draw us closer to Himself.

But what strange wrappings cover those heaven-sent gifts!

He leads us to give so that we might receive…He allows loneliness

that we might find ourselves in new and unexpected friendships…

and He permits difficult circumstances that we might look

past the glitter and tinsel of lesser gifts to find

those that will last forever.

James Dobson

A Christmas WORLD

In 1918, the Birdsall family lived near the corner of Griffith Avenue and Washington Boulevard on the east side of Los Angeles. There were then only four of us: Pop, Mom, Helen, and me, Bergen. We must have been poor, because each Christmas and Thanksgiving, big baskets of food were left at our door. Come to think of it, we probably were poor, but we kids didn't seem to know it at the time.

BERGEN BIRDSALL

Come, let us bow down in worship,
let us kneel before the LORD our Maker;
for he is our God and we are the people of his pasture,
the flock under his care.

PSALM 95:6–7

37

My sister, Helen, at age ten was boss of all the kids along Griffith Avenue. It was Helen who decided where we would go, what we would play, and who we would allow to go or play with us. Helen was the decision maker. She was also the storyteller, the energizer, the jokester. Helen was the champion of the new kid who didn't belong. Nobody put down anybody around Helen.

Seated regally in her buggy, Helen ruled the Griffith Avenue gang. A baby buggy at ten years of age? No, not a baby buggy— this was a transportation buggy. Helen could not walk. She had to be pushed wherever she needed or wanted to go. Push power? No problem: every child and most adults for blocks around considered it a privilege

to push. And if there were no others around, there was always good old Bergen. We made a great pair. Helen had the brain; I had the brawn. Helen made the decisions; I did as I was told. Turn right. Turn left. Go faster. Go slower. Stop.

Christmas in Southern California can often be warm, sometimes hot, almost always pleasant enough to walk around barefoot, particularly if you are eight going on nine. So it was barefoot Buggy Pusher who prudently nodded assent when Queen Helen proposed early in December: "Let's take all our money and go downtown and buy Mom a vase for Christmas." (Helen had recently heard a preacher from England and she said 'vahz' the way he did.) "Do you agree?"

Of course I agreed. I always did. Helen had never taken a course in how to influence people, but she knew the principles of manipulating younger brothers: make 'em think they're in on the decision making.

"Where shall we go?" Go? There was only one place in all Los Angeles—the very best store in town. I knew where that was. We'd never been brash enough to actually walk into Blackstone's Department Store, but every time we passed the corner of Ninth and Broadway we wondered what cornucopia of delights might be on display behind those elegant doors. "Where will we get the money?"

"Don't worry about the money; we've got seventy-nine cents in our savings, and we'll spend it all. I know just what we want!" Helen's "we" was a euphemism for "I," but it made Little Brother feel he was in on the act.

The Saturday before Christmas, we made our twenty-one-block pilgrimage to Blackstone's. In those halcyon days, the best department stores boasted doormen, each resplendent in a colorful uniform, epaulets, gold braid, brass buttons, shiny black boots, and a big smile. Oh, it was grand to have so important a person open the door for you. They did it even for an eight-year-old barefoot boy pushing a ten-year-old girl in a buggy.

That carpet! How it caressed the soles of our feet. No wonder people loved to shop at Blackstone's. Those salesgirls—all in shiny black satin with white collars and cuffs. Those

intriguing bells bonging away with gentle insistence, probably trying to get Mr. Blackstone's attention. Those fascinating cash boxes rattling mysteriously across the store all by themselves from clerk to cashier and back. Those floorwalkers meticulously dressed in striped trousers, cutaway coat, white gardenia—and a frown. That floorwalker! "What do you two dirty kids want in this store? Just look at our carpet. Get that buggy out of here, and don't you ever come back!"

"All right, Bergen, do what the man says," Helen said. But when we reached the door, she ordered, "Now, Bergen, turn the buggy around." Looking back up into the frowning faces of Blackstone's best, Helen told them: "First of all, yes, we are kids, but we are not dirty kids. Second, it didn't hurt your old carpet to have a little dust from our bare feet on it, and you can get all those wheel marks out easy with a Bissell sweeper. But my brother and I want you to know that as long as we live, we'll never come into Blackstone's again." I'm not sure about this, but my guess is that the floorwalker was probably relieved to hear it.

"Now what shall we do?" I asked.

"Oh, that's easy, we'll go to the second best store in town." Seventh and Broadway: Bullock's Department Store. They, too, had a doorman. He wore epaulets, braid, brass, and boots. He smiled at us, but so had the Blackstone's doorman, so that didn't mean much. Bullock's had a carpet, too, even though not the kind that caressed the bare foot. Their carpet had a short nap that mostly just tickled. Black satin, white collars, white cuffs, traveling cash boxes, call bells that ping-ponged around the store—probably calling Mr. Bullock. Floorwalkers with striped trousers, cutaway coat, and gardenia.

That floorwalker! With a smile, he asked courteously: "And what can we do for you two young people?" Young people, mind you, not "dirty kids."

"My brother and I would like to go to the seventy-nine-cent 'vahz' department."

"It's on the fourth floor. Please follow me to the elevator."

Now, the elevators in 1918 were not your present-day sterile plastic cages with impersonal push buttons and brilliant fluorescent lights. They were fashioned of intricately woven black iron with open lattice-work doors and sides. They were manned by uniformed operators who skillfully pushed the bright-handled levers to move the car. After a slight pause, the cage would start up with a bounce and a swoosh of hydraulic fluid that provided the power. When the elevator reached a floor, it didn't stop right on target; it often needed just a wee smidgen up or a wee smidgen down. The door rattled open, then clinked shut.

"Fourth floor! The seventy-nine-cent 'vahz' department is over there in that little alcove." And then began a long parade of salespersons bringing an amazing array of vases in shapes, colors, and sizes to bedazzle anyone, even ten-year-old Queen Helen of Griffith Avenue and her Gentleman-in-Waiting. The surprising thing was that not one of the vases cost more than seventy-nine cents. The choice was narrowed to two when all of a sudden I looked around and demanded: "Where is our buggy?" I was only

eight, but I was still the man of the party, and the buggy was my responsibility.

Just then, in rolled Helen's Buggy, sparkling with brand-new rubber-tired red wheels, a new red wooden handle, and new leatherette seat and back cushion. All the trim was polished and shining. Such a buggy may have been seen before in Bullock's, but certainly never on Griffith Avenue.

"My brother and I have decided to buy this 'vahz,'" Helen announced, pointing to what surely must have been the most expensive vase of all. "Gift wrap it, please."

Out of the alcove, back to the elevator, down to the street floor, toward the big front

door, accompanied by a growing entourage of salesclerks, floorwalkers, buyers, shoppers, maintenance crew members, and the just plain curious.

When we reached the door, Helen ordered: "Bergen, turn the buggy around." Looking as if she were about to bestow knighthood upon the floorwalker, Queen Helen said: "My brother and I want you to know that we know very well that this vase cost a lot more than seventy-nine cents." (In her excitement, Helen slipped back into the vernacular.) "We know there could not possibly be enough money left over to fix up our buggy the way you did. My brother and I also want you to know that as long as we live, we'll never forget what Bullock's did for us today."

On our way home, downtown Los Angeles wasn't just a busy city crowded with Christmas shoppers. It was a beautiful world where adults treated children like people. It was a Christmas world as we began to understand the joy of giving, the joy of receiving.

"WHOEVER WELCOMES ONE *of these little*

children in my name welcomes me; and whoever welcomes me

does not welcome me but the one who sent me."

(MARK 9:37)

God's own Son took a little boy into His arms, and declared to the ages:

"Let the little children come to me, and do not hinder them,

for the kingdom of God belongs to such as these."

(MARK 10:14)

"A Christmas world" is a place where no one is too busy

or important to welcome a little child. Most likely, the sales staff at

Bullock's had many other customers and plenty of things to do

on that hectic shopping day so long ago. But when they opened their doors

to a barefoot lad and a disabled little girl clutching seventy-nine cents,

they welcomed the King of Glory, unawares.

— ❧ —

James Dobson

If You're
MISSING BABY JESUS

JEAN
GIETZEN

In the depths of a bitterly cold December, my mother decided it simply wouldn't do to go through the holidays without a nativity set.

It was 1943, in a small town in North Dakota. My father worked for an oil company during my growing-up years, and we'd moved around to several different parts of the state with his job. At some point between one move and another, we lost our family's little manger scene.

*"Today in the town of David a Savior
has been born to you; he is Christ the Lord.
This will be a sign to you: You will find a baby
wrapped in cloths and lying in a manger."*

LUKE 2:11–12

45

Happily, Mother found another at our local five-and-dime for only $3.99. When my brother and I helped her unpack the set, however, we found two figurines of the baby Jesus.

Mother frowned, "Someone must have packed this wrong," she said, counting out the pieces. "We have one Joseph, one Mary, three wise men, three shepherds, two lambs, a donkey, a cow, an angel—and two babies. Oh, dear! I suppose some set down at the store is missing a baby Jesus."

"Hey, that's great, Mom," my brother said with a laugh. "Now we have twins!"

Mother wouldn't have a bit of it. "You two run right back down to the store and tell the manager that we have an extra Jesus."

"Ah, Mom."

"Go on with you now. Tell him to put a sign on the remaining boxes saying that if a set is missing a baby Jesus, call 7162."

She smiled. "I'll give you each a penny for some candy. And don't forget your mufflers. It's freezing cold out there."

The manager copied down my mother's message, and sure enough, the next time we were in the store we saw his cardboard sign:

If you're missing baby Jesus, call 7162.

All week long we waited for the call to come. Surely, we thought, someone was missing that important figurine.

What was a nativity set without the main attraction? Each time the phone rang, my mother would say, "I'll bet that's about Jesus."

But it never was.

With increasing exasperation, my father tried to explain that the figurine could be missing from a set anywhere—Minot, Fargo, or even Walla Walla, Washington, for that matter. After all, packing errors occurred all the time. He suggested we just put the extra Jesus back in the box and forget about it.

"Back in the box!" I wailed. "What a terrible thing to do to the baby Jesus. And at Christmastime, too."

"Someone will surely call," my mother

reasoned. "We'll just keep the babies together in the manger until we find the owner."

That made my brother and me happy. It was special to look into that little manger and see two Christ children, side by side, gazing up into the adoring eyes of Mary. And was that a surprised look on Joseph's face?

But the days went by, and no one called. When we still hadn't heard from anyone by five o'clock on Christmas Eve, my mother insisted that Daddy "just run down to the store" to see if there were any sets left.

"You can see them right through the window, over on the counter," she said. "If they're all gone, I'll know someone is bound to call tonight."

"Run down to the store?" my father thundered. "Ethel, it's fifteen below zero out there!"

"Oh, Daddy," I said, "we'll go with you. Won't we, Tommy?" Tommy nodded vigorously. "We'll bundle up good. And...we can look at all the decorations on the way."

My father blew out a long sigh and headed for the front closet. "I can't believe I'm doing this," he muttered. "Every time the phone rings everybody yells at me to see if it's about Jesus. And now I'm going off on the coldest night of the year to peek in some store window to see if He's there or not there."

Daddy muttered all the way down the block in the cold, still air, while my brother and I raced each other to the store. The streets were empty and silent. But behind each lighted window, we knew that families were gathering around Christmas trees and manger scenes and fireplaces and tables laden with tasty holiday treats.

I was the first to reach the store window, where colored lights flickered along the edge of the frosty pane. Pushing my nose up against the glass, I peered into the darkened store.

"They're all gone, Daddy!" I yelled. "Every set must be sold."

"Hooray!" my brother cheered, catching up with me. "The mystery will be solved tonight!"

My father, who had seen no logical reason to run, remained some yards behind us. When he heard our tidings, he turned on his heel and started for home.

Inside the house once more, we were

surprised to see only one baby Jesus in the manger. Where was the Twin? For that matter, where was Mother? Had she vanished, too?

Daddy was unperturbed. "Someone must have called," he reasoned, pulling off his boots. "She must have gone out to deliver the figurine. You kids get busy stringing those popcorn strands for the tree, and I'll wrap your mother's present."

We had almost completed one strand when the phone rang. "You get it, Jean," my father called. "Tell 'em we already found a home for Jesus!"

My brother gave me a quick, eager look. Our mystery would be solved at last.

But the telephone call didn't solve any mystery at all. It created a much bigger one.

It was my mother on the phone, with instructions for us to come to 205 Chestnut Street immediately, and to bring three blankets, a box of cookies, and some milk.

My father was incredulous. "I can't believe this," he groaned, retrieving his boots for the second time that evening. "What in Sam Hill has she gotten us into?" He paused. "205

Chestnut. Why, that's eight blocks away. Wrap that milk up good in the blankets or it'll turn to ice by the time we get there. Why in the name of heaven can't we get on with Christmas? It's prob'ly twenty below out there now. And the wind's pickin' up. Of all the crazy things to do on a night like this."

Tommy and I didn't mind at all. It was Christmas Eve, and we were in the middle of an adventure. We sang carols at the top of our lungs all the way to Chestnut Street. My father, carrying his bundle of blankets, milk, and cookies, looked for all the world like Saint Nicholas with his arms full of goodies.

My brother called back to him. "Hey Dad, let's pretend we're looking for a place to stay—just like Joseph 'n' Mary."

"Let's pretend we're in Bethlehem where it's probably sixty-five degrees in the shade right now," my father answered.

The house at 205 Chestnut turned out to be the darkest one on the block. One tiny light burned in the living room, and the moment we set foot on the front porch steps, my mother opened the door and shouted, "They're here,

WHAT SWEET MUSIC...

can we bring,

than a carol for to sing,

the birth of this our heavenly King?

Awake the voice!

Awake the string!

Heart, ear, eye, and everything!

ROBERT HERRICK

they're here! Oh, thank God you got here, Ray! You kids take those blankets into the living room and wrap up the little ones on the couch. I'll take the milk and cookies."

"Ethel, would you mind telling me what's going on here?" my father huffed. "We've just hiked through sub-zero weather with the wind in our faces all the way—"

"Never mind all that now," my mother interrupted. "There's no heat in this house, and this young mother doesn't know what to do. Her husband walked out on her. Those poor little children will have a very bleak Christmas, so don't you complain. I told her you could fix that oil furnace in a jiffy."

Well, that stopped my father right in his tracks.

My mother strode off to the kitchen to warm the milk, while my brother and I wrapped up the five little children who huddled together on the couch. The distraught young mother, wringing her hands, explained to my father that her husband had run off, taking bedding, clothing, and almost every piece of furniture. But she'd been doing all right, she explained, until the furnace broke down.

"I been doin' washin' and ironin' for folks, and cleanin' the five 'n' dime," she said. "I—I saw your number every day there, on those boxes on the counter. Then—when the furnace went out—that number kept goin' through my mind. 7162. 7162.

"Said on the box that if a person was missin' Jesus, they should call you. That's how I knew you was good Christian people, willin' to help folks. I figured that maybe you'd help me, too. So I stopped at the grocery store tonight and called your missus. I'm not missin' Jesus, mister, because I surely love the Lord. But I am missin' heat.

"Me and the kids ain't got no beddin',

and no warm clothes. I got a few Christmas toys for 'em, but I got no money to fix that furnace."

"It's okay," my father said gently. "You called the right number. Now, let's see here. You've got a little oil burner there in the dining room. Shouldn't be too hard to fix. Probably just a clogged flue. I'll look it over, see what it needs."

My mother came into the living room carrying a plate of cookies and a tray of cups with warm milk. As she set the cups down on the coffee table, I noticed the figure of the baby Jesus—our Twin—lying in the center of the table. There was no Mary or Joseph, no wise men or shepherds. Just Jesus.

The children stared wide-eyed with wonder at the plate of cookies my mother set before them. One of the littlest ones woke up and crawled out from under the blanket. Seeing all the strangers in his house, his face puckered up, and he began to cry. My mother swooped him in her arms and began to sing to him.

"This, this, is Christ the King

Whom shepherds guard and angels sing..." Mother crooned, while the child wailed. *"Haste, haste, to bring Him laud,*

the Babe, the son of Mary."

She went on singing, oblivious to the child's cries. She danced the baby around the room until finally, in spite of himself, he settled down again.

"You hear that, Chester?" the young woman said to another child. "That nice lady is singin' 'bout the Lord Jesus. He ain't ever gonna walk out on us. Why, He sent these people to us just to fix our furnace. And blankets—now we got blankets, too! Oh, we'll be warm tonight. Jesus saves, that's what He does."

My father, finishing his work on the oil burner, wiped his hands on his muffler. "I've got it going, ma'am, but you need more oil. I'll make a few calls tonight when I get home and we'll get you some.

"Yessir," he said with a sudden smile. "You called the right number."

When Daddy figured the furnace was going strong once more, our family bundled

up and made our way home under a clear, starry heaven. My father didn't say a thing about the cold weather. I could tell he was turning things around in his mind all the way home. As soon as we set foot inside the front door, he strode over to the telephone and dialed a number.

"Ed? This is Ray. How are ya? Yes, Merry Christmas to you, too. Say, Ed, we have kind of an unusual situation here tonight. I know you've got that pickup truck, and I was wonderin' if we could round up some of the boys and find a Christmas tree, you know, and a couple things for...."

The rest of the conversation was lost in a blur as my brother and I ran to our rooms and began pulling clothes out of our closets, and toys off our shelves.

My mother checked through our belongings for sizes, and selected some of the games she said "might do." Then she added some of her own sweaters and slacks to our stack.

It was a Christmas Eve like no other.

Instead of going to bed in a snug, warm house, dreaming of a pile of presents to open on Christmas morning, we were up way past our bedtime, wrapping gifts for a little family we'd only just met. The men my father had called found oil for the furnace, bedding, two chairs, and three lamps. They made two trips to 205 Chestnut before the night was done.

On the second trip, he let us go, too. Even though it must have been thirty below by then, my father let us ride in the back of the truck, with our gifts stacked all around us.

My brother's eyes danced in the starlight. Without saying anything, we both knew Christmas could never be the same after this. The extra Jesus in our home hadn't been ours to keep after all. He was for someone else...for a desperate family in a dark little house on Chestnut Street.

Someone who needed Jesus as much as we did.

And we got to take Him there.

"THE KING WILL REPLY, 'I tell you the truth, whatever you did for one of the least of these brothers of mine, you did for me.'"
(MATTHEW 25:40)

There is no higher privilege, no deeper joy, than to become Jesus Christ—if only for a moment—to someone who needs Him in a moment of trouble or deep distress.

It's more than just speaking or teaching about Him. It is actually stepping into His place, becoming His hands and feet. It is allowing Him to so fill your heart and empower your life that your touch becomes His touch…your voice becomes His voice…your compassion and mercy and tenderness become His, poured out to a hurting world.

And when we do these things…when we feed the hungry, take in a stranger, clothe the naked, or visit the sick or the prisoner in His name and His power, something mysterious happens. The King tells us, "You did that for Me. You touched My life, in My need, and I will remember it for eternity."

On a Christmas long ago, He came as a light into a hopeless world. Through our yielded, available lives, His love continues to push back the darkness.

— ❧ —

James Dobson

53

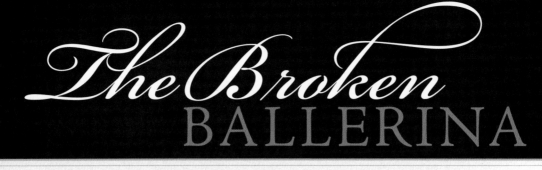

The Broken BALLERINA

"Silent Night" played from a low-volumed radio in the kitchen.

It was midnight, just a week before Christmas. Outside our

suburban home a blizzard raged. But set against the colonial

panes of our living room window, a glistening Christmas tree

lit the bitter night with glittery silver tinsel and strands of tiny

white lights.

My husband and three children were upstairs, fast asleep.

I snuggled into an armchair near the tree as I savored the late-

night silence of my home.

NANCY JO
SULLIVAN

*Moments
of Grace*

*We have peace with God through
our Lord Jesus Christ, through whom we have
gained access by faith into this grace
in which we now stand.*

ROMANS 5:1–2

It felt good to relax. That morning the kids had gotten up at 6:30 to decorate for the holidays. Most of our Christmas ornaments now hung in clusters on the tree, sideways and backwards and upside down. But I liked the way it looked. It's custom decorated, I thought.

As I began to doze, I heard the sound of soft, slippered footsteps coming down the stairs. I turned to find Sarah, my Down's syndrome daughter, standing on the landing. Dressed in a teddy bear print robe, she held a small cedarwood box, latched with gold hinges.

"M-M-Mommy…we f-forgot s-s-something today."

Though Sarah had just turned fourteen, she still bore a childlike sweetness. With a dimpled grin and curled ponytails, her hazel-green eyes sparkled through pink-framed glasses.

"You remembered," I said, as she nestled in next to me, setting the box on my lap. Together we opened it.

Inside were keepsakes I had saved since her birth: stacks of greeting cards, letters yellowed with age, baby photos of unforgettable days. Sarah ran her hand over a child's baseball mitt and a tiny pair of dancing slippers. Then she found what she was looking for, wrapped in tissue—a Christmas ornament, a tiny ballerina fashioned from delicate wood. I had bought it for her years earlier, just hours before she was born.

Once this ornament was a symbol of dreams surrendered; now it evoked images of a spiritual journey filled with tender, irrepressible lessons of faith.

As Sarah laid her head on my shoulder, I took the ornament into my hand and thought about the day that journey began.

In my mind, I traveled back in time to when I was a little girl. It was early Christmas morning, and it was snowing outside the

small Lake Superior home where my family lived.

As I tiptoed down our stairway, I saw my dad piling presents underneath the Christmas tree in our living room. He motioned me near. As I settled into his lap, he handed me a small package wrapped in shiny red foil.

Carefully ripping away the wrapping, I found to my delight a music box—royal blue and trimmed with colored spangles.

I opened it. From a mirrored ledge within, a ballerina, small and delicate, sprang up, her pink leotard glittering with ivory sequins, her lace net skirt gathered into a silver sash around her waist.

I watched in wonder as my father wound the box with a golden key. With each crank, the ballerina began to twirl, round and round to a tune that sounded like clock chimes. Enchanted, I dreamed that one day I would be a dancer too. But it was not to be.

More mental snapshots appeared in my mind's eye: the day my parents told me they couldn't afford dance lessons; the night I watched a middle-school friend perform in a recital that I wanted to be part of; the morning I learned that I had not made the final cut for our high school dance line. I even remembered a ballroom dance class I had taken in college. By that time I had learned to laugh my way through ungraceful glides and unmastered steps. At last it seemed I had dismissed the dancing visions of my youth.

But a few years later, on a sunny July morning, it seemed those snuffed-out dreams were beginning to rekindle.

That was the morning my husband Don and I arrived for an appointment at the obstetrics clinic. We were newlyweds and I was pregnant with our first child; our doctor had ordered a routine sonogram.

While we watched the movements of our unborn baby on the ultrasound monitor, we were utterly amazed. Our child seemed completely and impeccably formed, even though I was barely showing. As we ran our fingers along the screen, we traced the outline of a baby's hand, counting each finger. There was no sign or suspicion of a disability, only

LOVING FATHER,

Help us remember the birth of Jesus,

that we may share in the song of the angels,

the gladness of the shepherds,

and the worship of the wise men.

May the Christmas morning

make us happy to be Thy children,

and the Christmas evening bring us to our beds

with grateful thoughts, forgiving and forgiven,

for Jesus' sake.

Amen!

ROBERT LOUIS STEVENSON

the steady sound of a strong heartbeat reverberating through the room.

"Looks like a girl," the doctor said. He had made the discovery incidentally, but for us it was a moment of tender, unexpected awareness. This was our daughter. She was real. We would name her Sarah Marie, which means "God's princess."

In the months that followed, we made preparations to welcome her. Though we weren't making much money as first-year schoolteachers, we had enough in savings for a down payment on our first home: a vintage Cape Cod with worn window boxes and siding that needed repair.

With the extra funds Don earned as a baseball coach, we bought a new crib and redecorated the baby's room. While Don painted the walls, I stenciled dancing bears along the windowsills and sewed ruffled curtains from pink and white gingham.

As the summer wore on, my waistline expanded and I resigned myself to a wardrobe of plaid maternity tops and stretch-paneled pants. It seemed as if I grew bigger by the day, and Don and I bantered on and on about our baby.

Who would she grow up to be? A renowned surgeon? A famous musician? A bestselling author?

"She'll be the next Babe Ruth," Don teased as he came home one autumn day holding a toddler's baseball mitt. He had paid a quarter for it at a garage sale.

"She will dance," I replied with a smile, reminding him that I had more sophisti-cated plans for Sarah. "She will dance…" I whispered the words every time I felt the kicks and turns of my baby. Even late at night when I couldn't sleep, I envisioned the glittery costumes she would wear and the soft-ribboned slippers that would hang from a peg in her room. As I imagined her bowing in a circle of stage light, I prayed that God would bless the hopes I held.

Then, on a blustery November after-noon, when the first snow of the season fell, it seemed that God was gently affirming my prayers.

I had been Christmas shopping at the

mall. Passing store after store, I watched as merchants decked display windows with colored lights and red-berried garlands. Inside one shop, I saw a twelve-foot balsam fir adorned with hundreds of decorations. I decided to buy an ornament for the baby I would be cradling by Christmas.

From houses to hockey sticks to cookies and crayons, that tree held every ornament imaginable; beeswax candles, cinnamoned hearts, brown furry bears, angels, and stars.

As I reached to take a closer look at a red-ribboned stroller, I accidentally knocked a small ornament from the bottom branch onto the floor. Kneeling down, I picked up a tiny ballerina.

Her creator had crafted her simply with a white-painted face, two dotted eyes of blue, and a penciled line of red for a smile. She wore only a sleeveless smock trimmed with a lace ruffle, no sequins or sashes or slippers. Yet her form was elegant, almost regal, with arms arched upward in a pose that looked like praise.

I wondered if God was speaking to me.

Perhaps this ornament was a sign from heaven, a divine reassurance that all my childhood dreams would one day be redeemed in the dance of my daughter.

I handed the clerk a ten-dollar bill as she wrapped the ballerina in layers of gold tissue paper.

Suddenly, I felt pain. The initial stages of labor had arrived; I knew it intuitively. Hurriedly I zipped the ornament into my purse.

Later that night, at 9:46 P.M., Sarah Marie was born. Another forty-five minutes and we heard a knock on our recovery room door. My baseball-capped husband answered with Sarah tucked in his arms. It was our doctor.

"I'm sorry," he said in almost a whisper.

Still clad in his surgical blues, he sat down on a chair next to my bed. He clutched a clipboard scrawled with the notes of an undeniable diagnosis.

"We think your daughter has a genetic abnormality." He spoke of symptoms— flaccid muscles, delayed reactions, an extra chromosome.

"I believe she has Down's syndrome," he said softly.

Don took off his cap and hung his head. I squeezed his hand. We had made plans and dreamed dreams for a child much different than the one he was describing.

"There are support groups here at the hospital for parents of the handicapped," the doctor continued. As he handed us brochures and suggested resources, I quietly repeated the words: "parents of the handicapped." It was an identity that demanded a surrendering of dreams.

I wanted to deny his findings. I wanted to say, "Recheck her, there's been a mistake,

she's fine." But somehow I knew that the diagnosis was true and that our lives had changed forever.

Midnight came. Late shift nurses set up an overnight cot for Don, right next to my bed. As I held Sarah in my arms, the lights in the maternity ward were dimmed and Don fell asleep.

In the faint glow of a bedside night-light, I looked in wonder at her newborn face. I searched for signs of a disability, but all I could find was the loveliness of a little girl. For her eyelashes were long and curled, her skin was soft and blushed, and her left cheek was sweetly dimpled.

"My little ballerina," I said softly.

With misting eyes, I reached for my leather bag. Unzipping it, I searched for a Kleenex, but wedged between my wallet and car keys I found instead the tissue-wrapped ornament.

I lifted the covered keepsake into my hand and peeled away each layer of wrapping.

The ballerina was broken.

"M-M-Mommy" Sarah said as she nudged

my arm, prying me away from the memories I had filed under "unforgettable."

"L-L-Look," she said.

I watched as my daughter sifted through old childhood photos, snapshots of Sarah riding a bike or chasing a butterfly or throwing a baseball to Don. Every picture had captured her smiling. Throughout the years, the challenges of her disability had been overshadowed by the immeasurable joy she had brought to our lives.

"M-My f-f-favorite," Sarah said as she held a photo I had taken just a few weeks earlier, a picture of Sarah standing on stage in a glittery dance costume.

For the last decade, Sarah had taken dance lessons at a studio called "Uniquely Able." She had learned how to dance, and our family had attended every recital.

As I looked at the photo, it occurred to me that Sarah had taught me the dance of faith.

Because of her, I had learned how to hold on to the hand of God, the strong steady hand that guides us through our unexpected losses, the gentle hand that lovingly twirls us to the other side of our broken dreams.

On that other side I had discovered, much to my delight, the irrepressible blessings of surrender and acceptance; I had uncovered the wondrous plan of God.

As I closed the lid on the cedar box, I placed the ballerina ornament in Sarah's hand.

"Go ahead," I said, motioning for Sarah to hang the ornament on our tree. Every holiday, this was her honored task.

As she ran her hands over the glue that had long since dried over the wood of the ballerina's arm, her eyes sparkled with happiness.

"She's not broken anymore," Sarah said.

Together, the two of us placed the ballerina on the highest branch of the tree, instead of a star.

"Not anymore." I said.

WHEN TREASURED DREAMS CRACK *and splinter,*

when high expectations and carefully laid plans wash

away like castles of sand, we wonder if we can live

with the brokenness left behind.

But the hand of God has skill beyond imagination.

From the ruins of a dream, He builds anew.

From disappointments and desolations, He crafts tender moments,

vulnerable hearts, and unforgettable memories.

When God mends a dream, it becomes a new creation.

Not, perhaps, what we thought we wanted…

but better than we could have ever conceived.

James Dobson

The Town That GAVE CHRISTMAS

It was Christmas Eve, 1927, in the remote prairie town of Hillspring, Alberta, Canada. Mary Thomas Jeppson was getting her six small children ready for bed. She thought her heart would break as she watched five of her children dance around the small house, excited to hang their socks for Santa to fill. Her oldest daughter, Ellen, sat subdued and sullen in a corner of the cold, two-room house. Ellen's heart was heavy for a ten-year-old, but she understood the reality of what tomorrow would bring. She felt that her mother was cruel to let the children get their hopes up when she knew very well there

MARIAN
JEPPSON
WALKER

*Christmas
Miracles*

We rejoice in the hope of the glory of God.

ROMANS 5:2

would be nothing to fill the socks. They would be lucky to have a little mush for breakfast, as there was only a small amount of wheat and corn left. The winter had just started and already it was cold and harsh. The milk cow had died the week before from starvation and severe weather conditions, and the last two or three chickens had stopped laying eggs about a month before.

Mary helped each one of the children hang a little darned and mended sock. She tried to persuade Ellen to hang one, too, but Ellen just sat there, shaking her head and mumbling "Mom, don't do this. Don't pretend." After the socks had been hung, Mary read the Christmas story from the Bible, and then recited a few Christmas poems from memory—and memories of her own happy childhood living in the United States flooded her mind. She was the next to youngest of a very large and loving family. Although they'd been pioneers in a remote area of Idaho, her mother and father had made life—and especially Christmas—very exciting and memorable.

Before Ellen went to bed, she pleaded with her mother to tell the children the truth. Mary kissed her daughter good night, and whispered, "I can't, Ellen. Don't ask me why—I just can't tell them." It was almost midnight and the other children had been asleep for hours, and Mary's husband Leland had gone to bed, too, feeling like a broken man, like he had failed his family completely. Mary sat by the fire reading the Christmas story from the Bible over and over again. Her mind drifted to her plight here in this godforsaken land of ice and snow. It was the beginning of the Depression and her husband had heard wondrous stories about the unlimited opportunities of homesteading in Canada. After two years of not being able to find work in the United States and after a flood had destroyed their small home in Willard, Utah, he had decided to move his family to Canada. It seemed, however, that they were five or six years too late to cash in on the rumored opportunities. After several seasons of unusual weather conditions, most of their crops had frozen or failed.

In October, Mary had received a letter from her family back in Idaho, asking what they could do to help and what they could send the family for Christmas. Mary had put off her response—she had too much pride to let them know how destitute her family really was. Finally in November, realizing that things were not going to get any better, she had written. She only mentioned the necessities. She told them how desperately they needed food, especially wheat, yeast, flour, and cornmeal. She related how long it had been since she had been able to bake a cake or cookies, because they had no molasses or honey, and of course, no sugar. It had been a year since they'd had any salt to use on their food. She also added that it would be wonderful if they could ship just a little bit of coal, because of the cold, and because their fuel supply was almost depleted. She finished her letter with a request for some old, used quilts. All of hers had worn thin and were full of holes and it was difficult keeping the children warm. She mentioned their need for anything to keep them warm—any used socks, shoes or gloves, warm hats or coats.

And at the very end of the letter she wrote, "If you could just find a dress that someone has outgrown that I could make over to fit Ellen, please send that, too. Ellen is such a little old lady for such a young girl. She carries the worries of the whole family on her thin shoulders. She has only one dress that she wears all the time, and it is patched and faded. She has outgrown it, and I would like so very much to fix up something that is nicer for her."

The week before Christmas, Leland hitched up the horse and sleigh and made the three-hour round trip from Hillspring

into the town of Cardston every day to check at the train station and post office whether a package had come from their family in Idaho. Each day, he received the same disappointing answer. Finally, on the day before Christmas, he went into Cardston first thing in the morning and eagerly waited for the mail delivery. He left in the early afternoon to get home before dark, and he left empty-handed. He wept openly as he rode home, knowing he would have to explain to Mary that perhaps the package would arrive the day after Christmas or the next week, but that it had not made it in time for the big day.

Mary suddenly awoke from her reminiscent sleep with a chill. The old clock on the wall said it was 3:30 A.M. The fire in the stove was all but out and she decided to add

a little more fuel so that it wouldn't take so long to start in the morning. She looked over at the little limp socks still hanging by the fireplace and felt a similar emptiness in her heart. Outside, the wind was blowing at about seventy miles per hour—the snowstorm had intensified.

Mary was about to put out the lantern and go to bed for a few short hours, when she heard a quiet knock at the door. She opened the door to find a man standing there, and in all her life she had never seen anyone look more like her vision of Santa Claus. He was covered with ice and snow and had a long beard, made white from the snow. His hat, his gloves, and boots were also white, and for a moment Mary thought she was dreaming.

It was the mailman, Mr. Scow from Cardston, who had known the plight of the Jeppson family. He told her that he knew they had been waiting for packages from Idaho and he knew there would be no Christmas without them. That evening, as he was finishing up a long day of delivering

IT CAME UPON A MIDNIGHT CLEAR,

That glorious song of old,

From angels bending near the earth

To touch their harps of gold.

"PEACE ON EARTH, GOOD WILL TO MEN,

From heaven's all gracious King!"

The world in solemn stillness lay

To hear the angels sing.

E. H. SEARS

mail all around the town, he was glad to be going home. His horse was exhausted and frozen as that day there had been one of the worst blizzards of the year. He was relieved to put his horse in the barn, park his sleigh, and return to the warmth of Christmas Eve at home with his family. But just as he was leaving, someone from the train station came running up to him and told him that ten large crates had just arrived from the States for the Jeppson family. It was only about four in the afternoon, but already it was dark and the storm was getting worse. They both decided there was nothing they could do about delivering the crates that night, but that they would be sure the Jeppsons received them the day after Christmas.

The mailman told Mary that when he went home, he had a disturbing feeling, and after discussing it with his wife, they decided that he needed to deliver the crates that night. He would have to find someone who would let him borrow a fresh horse and a sleigh with sharp running blades. After he finished telling Mary about his decision to

come, he brought the crates into the house. She insisted that he thaw out and warm up by the stove while she went out to check on his horse. When she looked at the poor animal with icicles hanging from its nose and mouth, she knew it would never make the trip back to Cardston that night and she tried to talk Mr. Scow into staying until morning. He refused the offer, telling her that it had taken him almost eight hours to make the trip to her house in the storm, and if he were to leave now, he would still be able to spend Christmas afternoon with his family. So Mary told him she would harness their own horse, which was in better condition, to make the trip back. She got him some dry clothes, fed him what warm food she could muster, and he headed off to town. It was almost 5 A.M., and he probably wouldn't get home until around noon.

Mary had thanked him as best she could, but for her whole life she maintained that there would never be sufficient words to express her gratitude. "After all," she would

say, "how do you thank someone for a miracle…and a Christmas miracle at that?"

As soon as he left, Mary began to unpack the crates. She only had an hour or so before the children would awaken. At the top of one of the crates she found a letter from her sisters. As she began to read the incredible account, tears streamed down her face. They told her that quilting bees had been held all over the Malad Valley, and from these, six thick, warm, beautiful quilts were included. They told her of the many women who had sewn shirts for the boys and dresses for the

girls, and of others who had knitted the warm gloves and hats. The donation of socks and shoes had come from people from miles around. The local church had even held a bazaar to raise the money to buy new coats and scarves for the whole family. All of the sisters, nieces and cousins, aunts and uncles had gathered to bake the breads and make the candy. There was even a crate half full of beef that had been cured and packed so that it could be shipped, along with two or three slabs of bacon and two hams.

At the close of the letter, her sisters said, "We hope you have a merry Christmas, and thank you so much for making our Christmas the best one we've ever had!"

When Mary's family awoke that Christmas morning, they did so to the sound of bacon sizzling on the stove and the smell of hot cinnamon muffins coming from the little oven. There were bottles of syrup and jars of jam, and canned fruit, including kinds that the youngest children had never seen before. Every sock that was hanging was stuffed with homemade taffy, fudge, divinity,

and dried fruit of every kind. The children didn't even know the names of some of the cookies and goodies that lay before them. Later, Mary and Leland were to find tucked in each toe of the stockings that had been sent for them a few dollars and a note stating that the money was to be used to buy coal and fuel for the rest of the winter, and oats and wheat to feed the animals.

For each boy there was a bag of marbles, and each girl had a little rag doll made just for her. But the most wonderful moment of the whole day was when Ellen awoke, the last to get up, and walked over to the spot where she had refused to hang her sock the night before. She rubbed her eyes in disbelief as she saw hanging there a beautiful red Christmas dress, trimmed with white and green satin ribbons. Ellen turned around, walked back to her bed, and lay down, thinking she was dreaming. After her little sisters pounced on her with laughter and excitement, she came back again to the celebration and joy of the most wonderful Christmas ever. For that morning, along with the aroma of good food, the love of a good family, and a new red dress, a childhood had been given back to a young girl—a childhood of hopes, of dreams, and of the wonder of Christmas.

I will never forget the retelling of this story by my mother, Mary Thomas Jeppson. Although it was always an emotional drain for her, it was an inspiration to all of those who were privileged to hear her story every Christmas since that magical day in 1927.

IN THE COURSE OF OUR LIVES, *so much passes through our hands. Money, checks, and bills. Keys to cars, deeds to homes, letters from friends well remembered and friends half-forgotten. But no matter whatever else slips through our fingers, we must never lose our grip on hope.*

We need hope. As those who belong to Jesus Christ, we understand that hope is more than positive mental attitude or a vague, wistful longing for better times. Hope is a Person, with a strong, warm grip and compassionate eyes. Hope is Someone who loves us with incredible passion, and refuses to surrender us to the dark designs of a passing world. Hope was born on a silent night in a village called Bethlehem, died on a Roman cross, and burst forth from the tomb three days later.

Hope is alive forevermore, brighter than the sunrise, scattering earth's darkest shadows. Reach for hope, and you will find Him. Keep Him for yourself, and give Him away.

Our very purpose in living rests in the blessed hope of Jesus. It will always be more than enough.

James Dobson

The Christmas STORY

Joseph also went up from Galilee, out of the city of Nazareth, into Judea, to the city of David, which is called Bethlehem, because he was of the house and lineage of David, to be registered with Mary, his betrothed wife, who was with child. So it was, that while they were there, the days were completed for her to be delivered. And she brought forth her firstborn Son, and wrapped Him in swaddling cloths, and laid Him in a manger, because there was no room for them in the inn.

Now there were in the same country shepherds living out in the fields, keeping watch over their flock by night. And behold, an angel of the Lord stood before them, and the glory of the Lord shone around them, and they were greatly afraid. Then the angel said to them, "Do not be afraid, for behold, I bring you good tidings of great joy which will be to all people. For there is born to you this day in the city of David a Savior, who is Christ the Lord. And this will be the sign to you: You will find a Babe wrapped in swaddling cloths, lying in a manger." And suddenly there was with the angel a multitude of the heavenly host praising God and saying: "Glory to God in the highest, And on earth peace, goodwill toward men!"

LUKE 2:4-14
(NKJV)

THE BIRTH OF A NEWBORN CHILD is a wondrous

moment—the appearance of a living gift that every mother and father

will love and cherish for as long as their days. Yet the birth of one

particular baby boy on an incredible night more than two thousand

years ago was a gift of even greater value, so meaningful and powerful

we can scarcely imagine it. For that miraculous event brought forth

a Savior, the holy and perfect Son of God, sent by our heavenly

Father to offer us the most important gift of all: everlasting life.

It has been my great privilege to assume the role of son, then

husband, and then father during my time on this earth. I have been

forever blessed by the presence of my parents, Shirley, and Danae

and Ryan in my life; words cannot fully describe the depth

of my love for each of these special people. It is overwhelming,

then, to consider that God's love for me is even greater than this.

Our heavenly Father cares for me—and for you—with an

infinite passion that is beyond our understanding:

"I have loved you with an everlasting love."

(JEREMIAH 31:3)

If you have never opened your heart to Jesus and joined

the eternal family of God, I invite you to do so this holiday season.

In a time of great giving, His is the most blessed of gifts!

Merry Christmas to you and your family. May this be

the most joyous season of all.

James Dobson

ACKNOWLEDGMENTS

"Delayed Delivery" by Cathy Miller. © 1993. Reprinted by permission of Joe Wheeler, Editorial Compiler of *Christmas in My Heart 2*, Review & Herald Publishing, and the author.

"Holy Awakenings at Christmas," taken from *Whispers from Heaven*, by Dayle Allen Shockley. © 1994. Dayle Shockley's work has appeared in dozens of publications. Her editorials and essays are regular features in *The Dallas Morning News*, and online at www.homebodies.org and www.NewsAndOpinions.com. Contact her at dshock@family.net. Used by permission of the author.

"Christmas Lost and Found" by Danae Dobson. © 1996. Used by permission of the author.

"A Christmas World" by Bergen Birdsall. Used by permission of Byron Birdsall.

"If You're Missing Baby Jesus" by Jean Gietzen. © 1999 by Multnomah Publishers, Inc. Used by permission of Multnomah Publishers, Inc.

"The Broken Ballerina," taken from *Moments of Grace*, by Nancy Jo Sullivan. © 2000 by Nancy Jo Sullivan. Used by permission of Multnomah Publishers, Inc.

"The Town That Gave Christmas" by Marian Jeppson Walker. © by Marian Jeppson Walker. Used by permission of William L. Walker.

ART INDEX

2-3	*Country Memories*
4	*Jingle Bells and Powder Snow*
8	*Village Carolers*
18	*A Time of Grace*
26	*Daddy's Priorities*
36	*The Bond of Faith*
44	*Wishes and Dreams*
54	*A Child's Delight*
64	*Heralding the Hope*
74	*Christmas in the Village*
78	*Memories of Home*
front cover	*Light Unto the World*
back cover	*Daddy's Priorities*
dedication page	*Three for Tea*